ignite your Fuego!

JOURNAL | MANIFEST | SET INTENTIONS

Ignite Your Fuego!

Coming into this world, who knew we would have the opportunity to meet great people who would challenge us to be our best selves, and show up fully in the spaces and places we create for ourselves. This is the experience Shauna, Lynda, and Jeanette share as they have spent most of their lives getting to know themselves, establishing their brands and creativity, and caring for their families. Fast forward to now in the world of cyberspace and online connections, The Heart of Chat was born!

Upon meeting and connecting, Shauna, Lynda, and Jeanette met in several online accountability and entrepreneur groups and built their brands around what they love. Love is the key word and igniting our fuego keeps us going and passionate about pursuing our dreams. Dreams really do come true and you must believe first in yourself, and then in your ability to pursue and fulfill your passion.

We invite you to this journal and embrace you while you are on your journey while you write down what makes you happy, the things that spark the fire in you, and going after what you desire in your life. Pour into these pages your thoughts and desires. Carry this journal with you to capture those candid thoughts and conversations in your mind. Remember to Pivot Pause Pour™ into yourself and love who you are. Your Fuego starts with you!

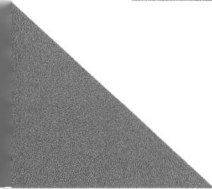

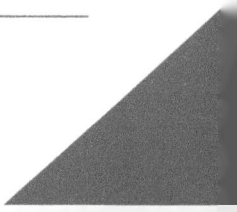

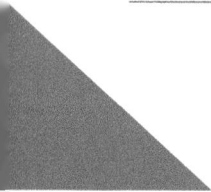

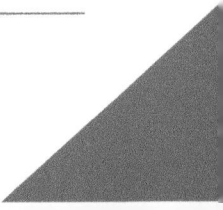

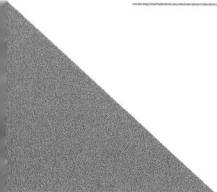

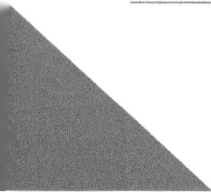

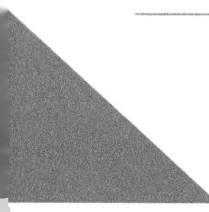

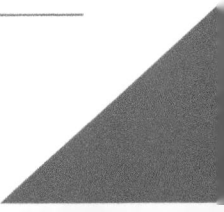

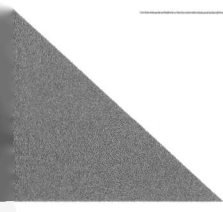

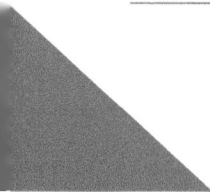

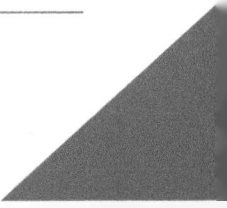

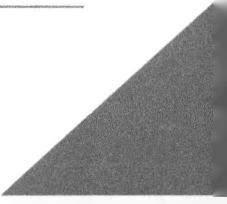

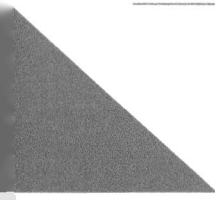

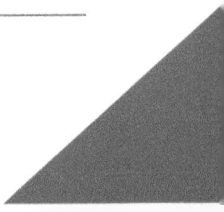

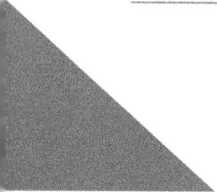

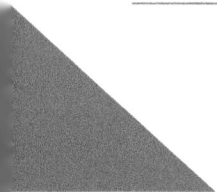

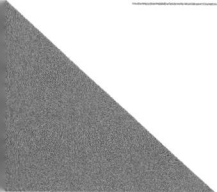

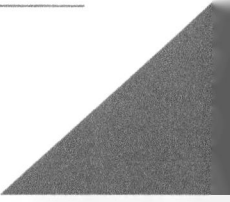

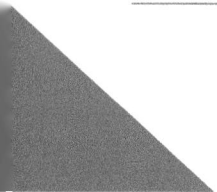

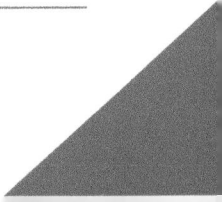

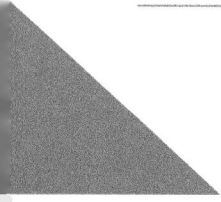

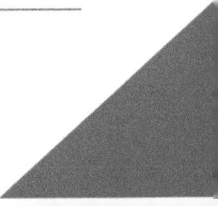

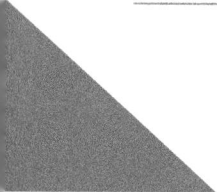

ignite your Fuego!

JOURNAL | MANIFEST | SET INTENTIONS

Hola to our Heartbeats!

I want to start by saying you are **incredible**, **resilient**, **capable**, **more than enough**, and a **positive light** that we need in this World. We all have special gifts and talents to bring to the table and know this, you are needed.

Being the best kept secret is no longer an option for anyone today. As we are all pivoting, pausing, and pouring into ourselves finding our voice is imperative. It's necessary to reach our full potential and capabilities to be the best version of ourselves daily. With this journal we hope through journaling, brain dumping, and **loving yourselves** you either continue on your positive journey, or use it for self discovery.

Lynda, Jeanette and I are passionate about self-discovery, finding your voice, and doing FUEGO WORK! Thank you for all of your love and support with The Heart of Chat. We care so much about everyone that supports us. You are our number one reason and motivation to keep all important life conversations going at The Heart of Chat.

Love + Strength,
Shauna

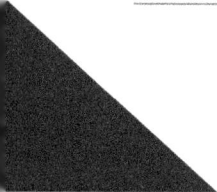

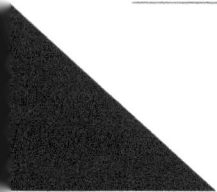

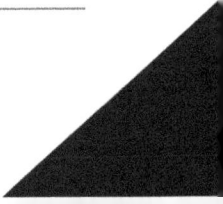

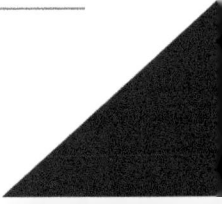

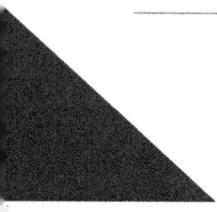

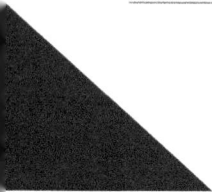

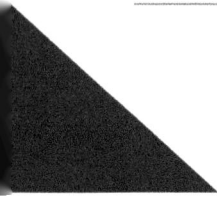

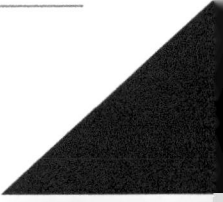

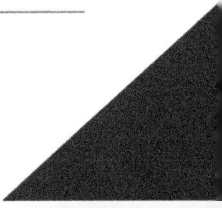

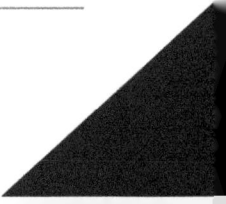

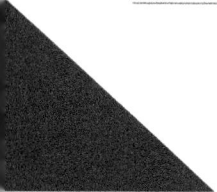

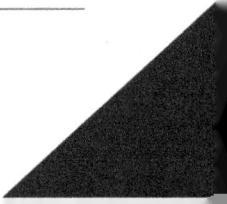

ignite your Fuego!

JOURNAL | MANIFEST | SET INTENTIONS

"You are Beautiful. You are Strong. You are Worth It."

This is my affirmation for you and one that I truly believe in. Believing in yourself and accepting who you are and who you aspire to be gives you all the permission you need to live life to the fullest.

Approaching life with positivity and turning obstacles into opportunities lets you know you can accomplish anything you set forth to do while you show up every day as your very best self.

Have the **Faith** to do what you **Love**. Your **Happiness** depends on you and the **Friendship** you have with yourself. Be **Honest** with yourself and possess **Integrity** in everything you do. **Trust** that you have what it takes to be happy and **Respect** the process that it takes to get there. **Openness** and **Acceptance** are two of the steps to get you there. **This is Your Life With A View.**

Love + Laughter,
Lynda

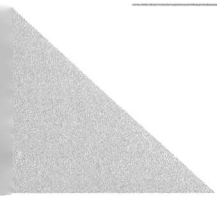

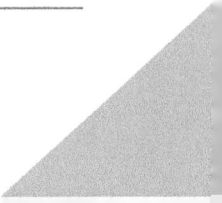

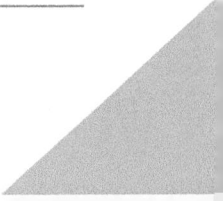

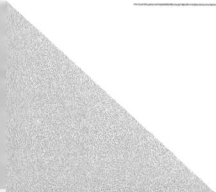

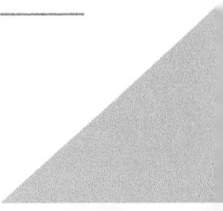

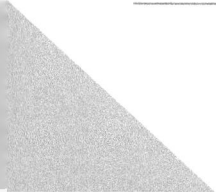

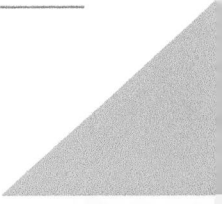

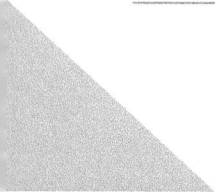

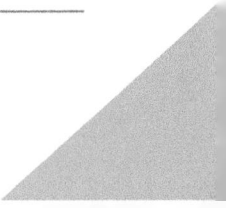

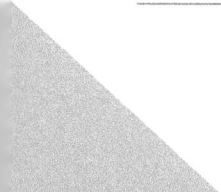

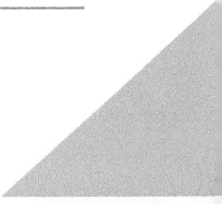

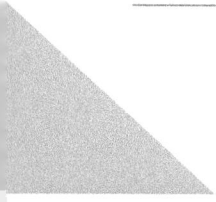

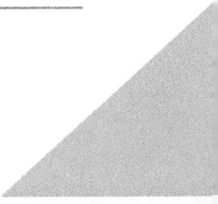

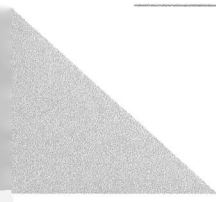

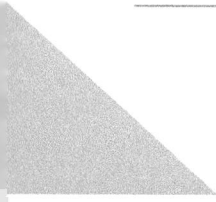

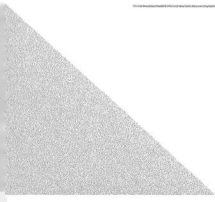

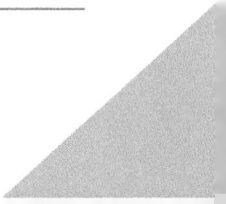

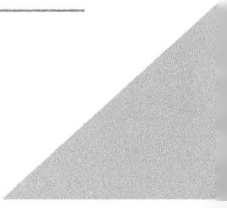

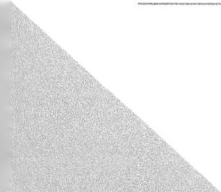

ignite your Fuego!

JOURNAL | MANIFEST | SET INTENTIONS

Through this journey of creating **The Heart of Chat** with Lynda & Shauna, I have allowed myself to trust and make space for my voice. My hope for you as you write in this journal is that you too find your voice. Finding your purpose and passion comes when you allow yourself to explore, experiment, dream, and more. Through these actions I pray you ignite a fire in you so strong that it burns up every negative thought and excuse.

Whatever your dreams are and wherever your passions lead, it all matters! It's all relevant to becoming the best version of yourself, for yourself! As long as you are doing it with "YOU" in mind. We have so many pressures in life to live and be what everyone else wants us to be. So why not live, do, and be all the things for yourself? You will never find yourself trying to be like someone else. Repeat after me, **I give myself permission to do what is right for me!**

When you are unsure, when you are experiencing extreme joy, when you are lost, and when you find yourself, document it in this journal and watch how you grow! **Watch As You Grow!**

Love + Joy,
Jeanette

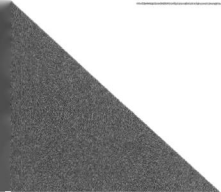

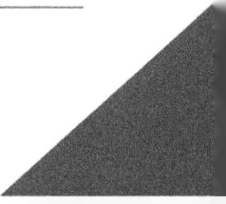

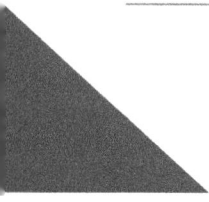

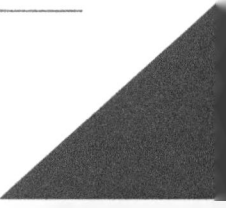

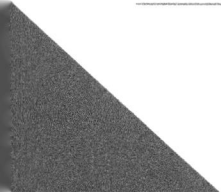

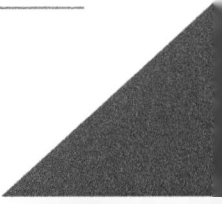

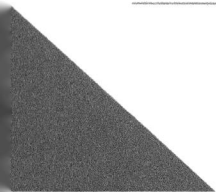

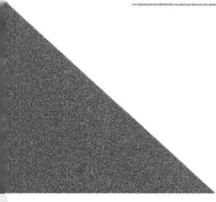

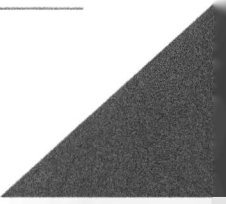

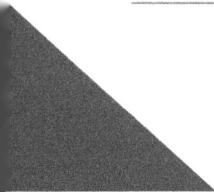

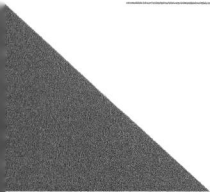

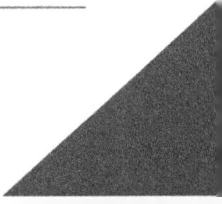

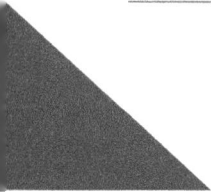

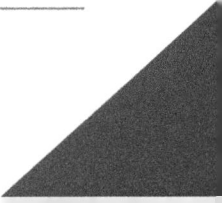

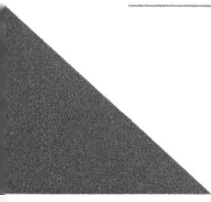

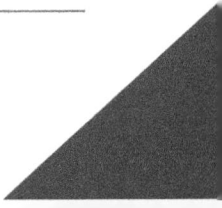

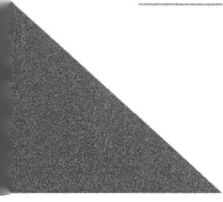

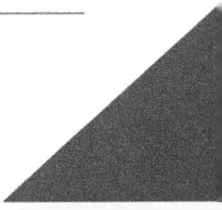

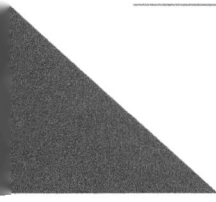

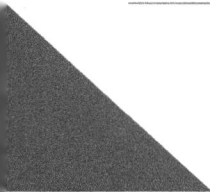

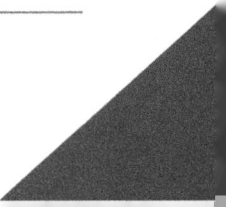

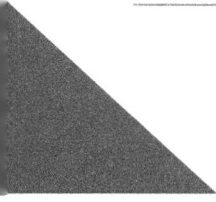

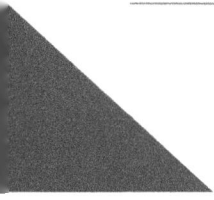

www.ingramcontent.com/pod-product-compliance
Lightning Source LLC
Chambersburg PA
CBHW040315100426
42811CB00012B/1449